STAR WARS™

REBEL HEROES

WRITTEN BY HANNAH DOLAN, ELIZABETH DOWSETT, CLARE HIBBERT, SHARI LAST, AND VICTORIA TAYLOR

INTRODUCTION

The Rebel Heroes are the saviours of the LEGO® *Star Wars* galaxy. Find out how they defeat the Empire with their clever disguises, powerful weapons, and incredible teamwork.

Introduction
MEET THE MINIFIGURES

HOW TO USE THIS BOOK

These amazing minifigures are ordered according to the *Star Wars*™ property in which they first appeared or mostly featured. Tabs at the top of each page indicate which properties this minifgure appears in. As most *Star Wars* characters appear in the wider universe of Legends, that tab is highlighted only if a minifigure appears in an Legends set. The Clone Wars tab has not been highlighted if the character has a separate Clone Wars minifigure.

This book also includes variants of featured minifigures, which are the same character, but have some modifications that make them different in some way.

Contents

This gutsy green Twi'lek is ready to make history! Hera Syndulla is one of the first minifigures in the new subtheme, LEGO *Star Wars* Rebels. Owner of the rebel starship the *Ghost*, she joins her rebel pals as they take on the evil Empire and travel the galaxy in pursuit of justice. Hera is exclusive to the 2014 LEGO® set, the *Ghost* (set 75053).

All smiles?
Hera has a double-sided head piece, with a neutral face on one side and a lopsided grin on the other.

Pilot helmet and flying goggles partly cover Hera's lekku

Hera Syndulla
REBEL PILOT

Unique face print on double-sided head-piece

Twi'leks
Hera is the fourth Twi'lek LEGO minifigure to be released. The others are Bib Fortuna, Oola, and Jedi Knight Aayla Secura.

Pilot jumpsuit and protective armor are unique printings

Lekku
Twi'leks are sometimes nicknamed "tail heads" because of their lekku (brain tails). Hera's lekku feature a white tattoo design.

DATA FILE

YEAR: 2014
FIRST SET: 75053 the *Ghost*
NO. OF SETS: 1
PIECES: 4
ACCESSORIES: Blaster

Hera conceals a secret blaster in her boot— just in case

Skin-colored head with grimacing face

Hair piece in unique color scheme—blue with orange streaks

Sabine Wren is one of the youngest rebels, but she already has an explosive reputation! This Mandalorian minifigure is skilled in blowing up key Imperial targets. She's also a grafitti artist, and loves to customize her armor and tag downed TIE fighters. Sometimes Sabine even combines her talents by planting paint bombs. She makes her debut in Ezra's Speeder Bike (set 75090).

About face
One side of Sabine's head piece has a concentrated expression for when she is carefully planting her explosives. Turn her head around and her battle face, with gritted teeth, comes into view.

Torso shows Mandalorian armor decorated with Sabine's own colorful designs

Bare arms allow her unrestricted movement

DATA FILE

YEAR: 2015
FIRST SET: 75090
Ezra's Speeder Bike
NO. OF SETS: 1
PIECES: 4
ACCESSORIES:
Twin blasters

Sabine Wren
EXPLOSIVES EXPERT

Twin blaster guns are easier to control than twin spraycans!

Tan legs have unique printing with chaps, gun belt, and graffiti on the knee pads

C1-10P, otherwise known as Chopper, is a stubborn little astromech droid who keeps all systems running aboard rebel starship the *Ghost*. Built mostly from second-hard parts, Chopper's minifigure has a uniquely small stature—smaller even than other LEGO *Star Wars* astromechs—thanks to his new, short leg and torso pieces. He beeps at crew members and saves the day in two sets.

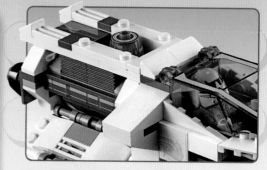

The *Phantom* and the *Ghost*
Chopper fits into the back of the *Phantom* attack shuttle, ready to guide rebel hero Zeb through battle. Chopper is always happy when the *Phantom* docks back safely to the larger starship, the *Ghost*.

C1-10P
ECCENTRIC ASTROMECH

DATA FILE

YEAR: 2014
FIRST SET: 75048
The *Phantom*
NO. OF SETS: 2
PIECES: 5
ACCESSORIES: None

Head piece is the same mold as other R5 minifigures, but with unique coloring and details

C1-series
Chopper is unique in LEGO *Star Wars*—as the only C1-series astromech minifigure. C1 droids are very old models, which perhaps explains why Chopper is so fond of "old-fashioned" starship maintenance.

Mechanical arms can zap enemies with an electroshock

Articulated arms extend from side compartments in Chopper's head

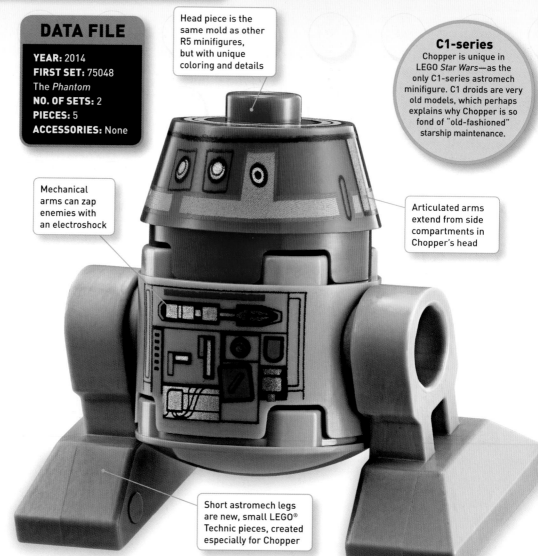

Short astromech legs are new, small LEGO® Technic pieces, created especially for Chopper

STAR VARIANT
Black hair

When Kanan's minifigure was first released in 2014, he had a black hair piece and printed black facial hair. His minifigure was later updated with brown hair to reflect Kanan's appearance on the TV show.

A former Jedi Padawan, Kanan Jarrus was forced into hiding following Order 66. Now he is a rebel leader and freedom fighter in two LEGO sets, the *Ghost* (set 75053) and Wookiee Gunship (75084). Kanan might be secretive about his Jedi past, but his minifigure's new ponytailed hair piece and bearded face show that he's not afraid to be unique.

Molded hair piece was specially designed for Kanan's minifigure

Lightsaber no longer needs to be hidden

Printed shoulder protector on unique torso

DATA FILE

YEAR: 2015
FIRST SET: 75084 Wookiee Gunship
NO. OF SETS: 1
PIECES: 4
ACCESSORIES: Lightsaber, blaster

Kanan Jarrus
JEDI IN HIDING

Blaster skills are enhanced by Kanan's Jedi training

Wookiee Gunship (set 75084)
Kanan joins Wullffwarro and the Wookiees aboard their gunship. Equipped with front cannons, rapid-fire shooters, and a mobile gun post, Kanan and his crew are ready for battle!

A fierce alien rebel from the planet Lasan, Zeb wants to end Imperial rule once and for all, with good reason—the Empire wiped out most of his species. Zeb joins the crew of the *Ghost* (set 75053) as their straight-talking gunner. He cuts a striking figure among his rebel friends with his purple skin, yellow battle suit, and unique head piece with bright green eyes.

Military man
Zeb is the only one of his rebel crew with military training, having been a member of the Lasan Honor Guard. He controls the *Ghost*'s rotating gun turret, and can't wait to launch an attack on the Empire!

Zeb
ALIEN ALLY

AB-75 bo-rifle
Part-blaster, part electrostaff, Zeb's bo-rifle weapon is built from two LEGO blasters connected by a lightsaber hilt piece.

Green eyes are a distinctive feature of the Lasat species

Goatee is a status symbol among the Lasat

Zeb has more powerful legs than humans

Belt and neck plate design continue on back of torso

DATA FILE

YEAR: 2014
FIRST SET: 75053
The *Ghost*
NO OF SETS: 1
PIECES: 3
ACCESSORIES: Bo-rifle

The *Phantom* (set 75048)

Ezra pilots the *Phantom*, a speedy attack shuttle that launches from the larger rebel ship, the *Ghost*. Ezra unfolds the wings and takes control of the two-way shooters. Stormtroopers, beware!

A Force-sensitive young thief from the planet Lothal, Ezra is surprised to find friendship among a group of rebels. He begins his Jedi training under the guidance of fellow rebel Kanan Jarrus (p.7). But instead of a standard lightsaber, gadget-loving Ezra carries one with a blaster built in to its hilt!

Helmet collector

Ezra has an unusual hobby: collecting Imperial helmets! His minifigure comes with a salvaged helmet in The *Phantom* (set 75048).

Lothal logo

The back of Ezra's torso is printed with a vintage logo—a remnant of Ezra's former life on the streets of Lothal.

Unique torso printed with pockets to hold Ezra's gadgets

Utility belt holds all sorts of gadgets

Knee pad and shin guard printed on leg pieces

Ezra Bridger
YOUNG REBEL

DATA FILE

YEAR: 2014
FIRST SET: 75048
The *Phantom*
NO OF SETS: 2
PIECES: 4
ACCESSORIES: Customized lightsaber

Brave astromech droid R2-D2 has ventured into 27 LEGO *Star Wars* sets to date, making him the most recurring minifigure in the LEGO line. R2-D2's head was redesigned in 2008, but the rest of his printing stayed the same until 2014. On Jabba's Sail Barge (sets 6210 and 75020), two different Artoos are forced to carry drinks on a tray built into his minifigure.

Astromech
When Artoo was released, his entire body was made from unique LEGO pieces. Since then, other astromechs have used the same pieces but with varying printing and colors.

STAR VARIANTS

Classic
The star of 14 sets from 1999 to 2008, the original R2-D2 has a white head with silver and blue printing.

New head
This variation with a light gray head appears in ten sets—the first is the Death Star (set 10188) in 2008.

R2-D2
ASTROMECH DROID

LEGO R2-D2 acquired a new bluish-gray head when he was redesigned in 2008

The 2013 R2-D2 in Ewok Village (set 10236) has lighter blue printing than this variant

Camera eye records messages

Holoprojector transmits holographic images and acts as a spotlight

DATA FILE

YEAR: 2014
FIRST SET: 75038 Jedi Interceptor
NO. OF SETS: 2
PIECES: 4
ACCESSORIES: None

LEGO Technic pins join legs to his body

Acoustic signaler

Ventilation point

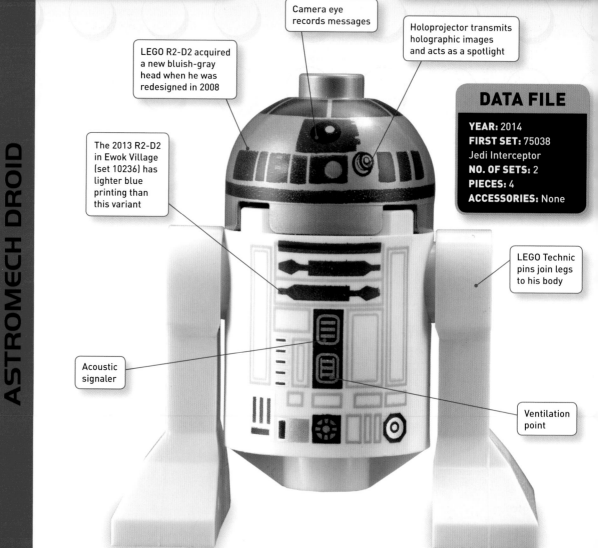

STAR VARIANTS

True original
The original C-3PO (left) appears in five sets between 2001 and 2005 in light pearl-gold. Two variants in richer pearl-gold, one with pale hands, appears in five more sets from 2008 to 2010.

Torso redesign
In 2012, C-3PO's torso was updated and given more detailed printing to show his colorful wiring. His legs remained plain gold.

Chrome gold
This limited-edition chrome gold C-3PO was randomly placed in 10,000 LEGO Star Wars sets to celebrate the 30th anniversary of Star Wars in 2007. The LEGO Group also made five of this minifigure in 14-carat gold.

Protocol droids
C-3PO was the first LEGO protocol droid and the original head-mold was specially cast for him. The LEGO Group went on to use the mold for other protocol droids, and the Death Star Droid.

Fretful C-3PO has found himself in 14 LEGO *Star Wars* sets since he was first released in 2001. The first LEGO *Star Wars* protocol droid, C-3PO now has six variants. All the ones up to 2012 have the same printing, but come in different tones of gold. Since 2012, C-3PO has new head and torso printing that shows his eyes, his colorful wires, an oil stain, and even the restraining bolt put on him by the Jawas.

Behind C-3PO
C-3PO's shiny gold armor continues on the back of his torso piece. You can also see his back plate and mid-body section.

Audiosensor— C-3PO has one on each side of his head

Warm gold arms and hands identical to 2012 variant's

C-3PO's connection wires are exposed in his mid-body section

DATA FILE
YEAR: 2014
FIRST SET: 75059 Sandcrawler
NO. OF SETS: 1
PIECES: 3
ACCESSORIES: None

C-3PO
PROTOCOL DROID

As a member of the Galactic Senate and secret sympathizer with the Rebel Alliance, Princess Leia Organa is a symbol of hope across the LEGO *Star Wars* galaxy. She dresses in the traditional white robes of the Alderaan royal family. Only one variant wears a cape—the ceremonial minifigure that is exclusive to the 2012 Gold Leader's Y-Wing Starfighter (set 9495).

STAR VARIANTS

Original Leia
A yellow-faced Leia flew into the LEGO *Star Wars* galaxy on the original *Millennium Falcon* (set 7190). A similar Leia with flesh-colored head and hands stars in four sets from 2007 to 2010.

Updated Leia
The Princess Leia minifigure was updated for the 2011 *Millennium Falcon* (set 7965). Her torso piece was given light bluish-gray printing.

Princess Leia
SENATOR OF ALDERAAN

Double-sided head was borrowed from Princess Tamina in LEGO® *Prince of Persia*

Leia is dressed up for an awards ceremony, where she will present pilot Dutch Vander with a medal

Leia probably stole this blaster from Imperial forces!

Serious side
First made in 2011, this double-sided Princess Leia head piece now features in six LEGO *Star Wars* sets.

Symbolic silver belt of Alderaan royalty

DATA FILE

YEAR: 2012
FIRST SET: 9495 Gold Leader's Y-wing Starfighter
NO. OF SETS: 1
PIECES: 5
ACCESSORIES: Blaster

STAR VARIANTS

First Luke

The young Luke variant with short tan hair and a yellow face and hands appears in three LEGO sets from 1999 to 2004. He also appears in LEGO Star Wars: *The Visual Dictionary* (2014) with updated printing.

Long locks

Ultimate Collector's *Millennium Falcon* (set 10179) comes with a Luke with feminine hair. There is a similar variant—but with white eye details—on Luke's Landspeeder (set 8092).

Mop head

The other side of the 2011 Luke's head has a printed blindfold for when he practices with his lightsaber. The same mop of hair appears on the smiling Luke given away at New York Comic-Con 2012.

Luke Skywalker is a poor farmboy who dreams of becoming a space pilot. He longs to escape the daily drudgery of life on his uncle's moisture farm. When he meets exiled Jedi Obi-Wan Kenobi, Luke's life changes forever and he finally has something to smile about. This smiling Luke appears in only three LEGO *Star Wars* sets.

DATA FILE

YEAR: 2014
FIRST SET:
75059 Sandcrawler
NO. OF SETS: 3
PIECES: 4
ACCESSORIES:
Blaster

Luke wore standard long female LEGO hair from 2007 until this hair was created for his 2011 redesign

Luke keeps farm tools in his brown utility belt pouch

Visual treat

The revised edition of DK's LEGO *Star Wars: Visual Dictionary* (2014) came with a Luke minifigure. An updated version of the first Luke minifigure, he had more creases printed on his shirt.

Unique leg piece has printed bindings to keep out the desert sand

Luke Skywalker
FARMBOY OF TATOOINE

Now an old man, Obi-Wan Kenobi is a Jedi in exile. He lives a hermit's existence on Tatooine and goes by the name of Ben Kenobi. But his minifigure shows signs of the life he once led: he wears Jedi robes and a brown cloak, and keeps his blue lightsaber close at hand. "Ben" Kenobi appears in seven LEGO *Star Wars* sets.

STAR VARIANTS

Original Obi-Wan The 1999 variant has a yellow head and hands and simple torso printing. In 2004 it was given new gray hair and printing, and in 2007 a flesh-colored version appeared.

Hood and cape Iin the *Millennium Falcon* (set 7965), Obi-Wan wears a hood and cape—the only other old Obi-Wan with these accessories is in the *Death Star* (set 10188).

Obi-Wan "Ben" Kenobi EXILED JEDI

Unique head with printed gray beard and wrinkles

White details in the eyes first appeared on a variant in Luke's Landspeeder (set 8092) in 2010

These dark brown and brick yellow robes are unique to the 2014 old Obi-Wan minifigure

A Jedi in exile, Obi-Wan still has his blue lightsaber

DATA FILE

YEAR: 2014
FIRST SET: 75052
Mos Eisley Cantina
NO. OF SETS: 1
PIECES: 4
ACCESSORIES:
Lightsaber

STAR VARIANTS

Original Wookiee

The first Chewbacca minifigure is made from the same pieces as the second variant, but they are all colored brown instead of reddish brown. The minifigure appears in three 2000–2001 sets.

Lucky for some

The second Chewie minifigure appears in 13 sets, from the 2004 *Millennium Falcon* (set 4504) to the 2013 *Ewok Village* (set 10236). The only printing of the head and body piece is for the nose and bandolier.

Comic-Con exclusive

In 2009, a handcuffed brown Chewbacca minifigure appeared in a collectible display set made exclusively for San Diego's Comic-Con, with Luke Skywalker and Han Solo minifigures in stormtrooper disguise.

Wookiee Chewbacca is a brave fighter and long-time companion of Han Solo. And just as Chewie towers over his friend in the *Star Wars* movies, his LEGO minifigure is notably taller than average. Chewbacca appears in 17 LEGO sets, ever ready to protect his home planet of Kashyyyk from invasion, or to fight alongside his rebel friends.

Unique printed, molded head

The head and textured body are made from a single piece that fits over a standard dark-brown minifigure torso

Bandolier contains energy bolts for the Wookiee bowcaster

DATA FILE

YEAR: 2014
FIRST SET: 75042
Droid Gunship
NO. OF SETS: 1
PIECES: 3
ACCESSORIES: Bowcaster

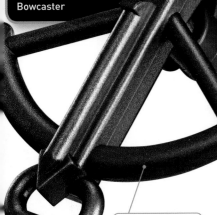

LEGO crossbow piece put to use as the distinctive Wookiee bowcaster

Legs printed with fur are unique to this Chewbacca minifigure

Chewbacca
WOOKIEE HERO

15

This bold minifigure is a loveable LEGO *Star Wars* rogue! The unlikely hero who found himself mixed up in the Rebellion against the Empire has now starred in 11 LEGO *Star Wars* sets. Like his beaten-up ship, the *Millennium Falcon*, Han's minifigure has been modified over the years—but he has retained his confident smile!

STAR VARIANTS

Three Solos

The original Han Solo (left) is very rare and comes in the first-ever LEGO *Millennium Falcon* (set 7190), released in 2000. A variant with brown legs was also released the same year. The starship's 2011 update (set 7965) is also piloted by an exclusive Han Solo (center). The right-hand variant has brown legs, a more detailed torso print and comes in two sets in 2013.

Han Solo
BRAVE BRAGGART

Millennium Falcon (set 75030)

This 2014 microfighter version of Han's battered YT-1300 light freighter features a mini cockpit for him to sit in. The speedy starship also has a quad laser cannon with two flick missiles to fire.

Since 2011, Han has had a flesh-colored head and white eye detailing

Harrison Ford

Han Solo is the first LEGO minifigure to be based on the likeness of actor Harrison Ford, who plays Han Solo in the *Star Wars* movies—but he is not the only one to be based on Ford! There is also a LEGO® Indiana Jones™.

Blue pants match Han's appearance in Episode IV, while his brown-legged variant represents Episode VI. All are printed with a belt for a blaster

DATA FILE

YEAR: 2014
FIRST SET: 75030
Millennium Falcon
NO. OF SETS: 2
PIECES: 4
ACCESSORIES: Blaster

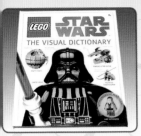

This Luke Skywalker minifigure was specially created to celebrate ten years of LEGO *Star Wars*. The minifigure himself has cause for celebration—Luke has been honored with a medal for bravery after destroying the first Death Star!

This long, tan LEGO hair is also seen on Tatooine Luke and Luke in his stormtrooper disguise

Book Luke
Luke with his medal of honor has not been seen in LEGO sets. It only appears in DK books, including LEGO Star Wars: *The Visual Dictionary* (2009).

Sparkling eyes
There is a second variant of the ceremonial Luke minifigure, which has white details on the eyes.

Pants pair
Luke is not the only minifigure to sport pants with a gun belt pattern. They are also worn by his friend Han Solo's minifigure. Han has worn the pants on Tatooine and Hoth.

Princess Leia Organa awards Luke with this medal of bravery for destroying the first Death Star at the Battle of Yavin

Luke might be celebrating, but he stays armed with this gun belt

Luke Skywalker
MEDAL WINNER

DATA FILE

YEAR: 2009
FIRST SET: LEGO Star Wars: *The Visual Dictionary*
NO. OF SETS: None
PIECES: 4
ACCESSORIES: None

This proud Han Solo minifigure is exclusive to the first release of this book! Han has received the highest medal of honor for his role in the destruction of the first Death Star. Cocky Han doesn't feel the need to dress up for the medal ceremony—what could look better than his cool blue jeans and black vest?

Fifth figure
This is the fifth version of Han Solo in LEGO form. The only LEGO *Star Wars* character available in more versions is Luke Skywalker, but three characters match Han Solo's number: Anakin Skywalker, Princess Leia, and Obi-Wan Kenobi.

Standard reddish-brown LEGO hair

The first release of this book in 2011 featured a Han Solo minifigure wearing his celebratory medal. The minifigure does not star in any LEGO sets

Han's unique torso features his favorite black waistcoat and light-colored shirt

Princess Leia Organa has awarded Han with this medal of honor for his heroics in the Battle of Yavin

Han Solo
DECORATED HERO

Lighter blue legs with a similar gun belt pattern are also seen on the regular Han Solo minifigure (p.16)

DATA FILE

YEAR: 2011
FIRST SET: LEGO *Star Wars: Character Encyclopedia*
NO. OF SETS: None
PIECES: 4
ACCESSORIES: None

18

Lando's head
This Lando Calrissian has a unique brown head with a suave slim mustache and winning smile! The two other versions of LEGO Lando have the same head piece in a reddish-brown color.

DATA FILE

YEAR: 2003
FIRST SET: 10123
Cloud City
NO. OF SETS: 1
PIECES: 5
ACCESSORIES: Blaster, cape

This cool customer is the baron administrator of Cloud City. Lando Calrissian has a flamboyant personality and sense of style—something that is reflected in his LEGO minifigure, with his extravagant yellow-lined cape and baronial outfit. Lando in all his finery only stars in the 2003 set Cloud City (set 10123), alongside his old gambling partner Han Solo.

The version of Lando dressed as a general has this same short black hair piece

Unique torso features a dark-blue collared shirt and matching baron administrator state belt

Blaster is made from a LEGO loudhailer piece

Lando's exclusive cape is blue on the outside and yellow on the inside. It is a status symbol that distinguishes him as baron administrator of Cloud City

Lando Calrissian
BARON OF CLOUD CITY

Half-man, half-robot,

Lobot is Lando Calrissian's cyborg assistant. Lobot's double-sided head is the only clue that he is not fully human: One side has a human face, while the other is printed with a computer implant. As Cloud City's computer liaison officer, Lobot is one of a kind—and so is his rare minifigure.

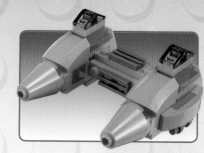

Twin-pod Cloud Car and Bespin (set 9678)
Lobot is the only minifigure to come with this LEGO *Star Wars* planet set. He uses the cloud car to run errands around Cloud City.

STAR VARIANT

In communication
This Lobot comes with the 2002 Twin-Pod Cloud Car (set 7119). Like his 2012 variant, he has a unique head that shows his implant. Instead of a blaster, however, he carries a radio.

Unusual behavior
It is only in a LEGO *Star Wars* set that Lobot would pilot a twin-pod cloud car. Usually, Lobot would leave the flying of vehicles to cloud car pilots, and focus on controlling the computer systems on Cloud City.

Unique head piece with wrinkle lines

Unique torso is printed with Lobot's plain, functional gray tunic, and black belt

Super computer
A computer device has been implanted into Lobot's brain. This allows him to control Cloud City's computer system with his mind.

Medium blaster

Lobot
CYBORG COMMAND CENTER

DATA FILE
YEAR: 2012
FIRST SET: 9678 Twin-pod Cloud Car & Bespin
NO. OF SETS: 1
PIECES: 3
ACCESSORIES: Blaster

Face of a princess
Underneath Boushh's helmet, Leia's head piece is immediately recognizable! It has been used for five other Princess Leia minifigures.

DATA FILE

YEAR: 2012
FIRST SET: 9516
Jabba's Palace
NO. OF SETS: 1
PIECES: 7
ACCESSORIES:
Lance blade, thermal detonator, hair

Lance blade for intimidation

Versatile princess
Princess Leia has appeared in 18 LEGO *Star Wars* sets in eight different guises, including her slave girl and Hoth outfits. This is her only minifigure that is in disguise.

Ubese clan belt clasp

Traditional tan-colored Ubese boots

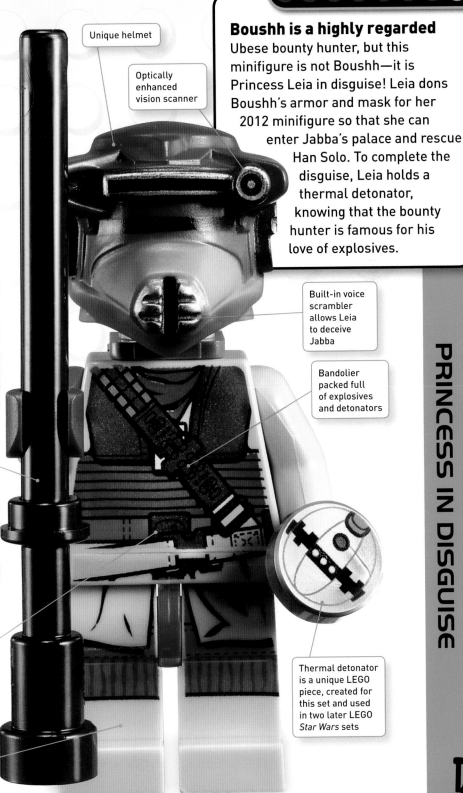

Unique helmet

Optically enhanced vision scanner

Boushh is a highly regarded Ubese bounty hunter, but this minifigure is not Boushh—it is Princess Leia in disguise! Leia dons Boushh's armor and mask for her 2012 minifigure so that she can enter Jabba's palace and rescue Han Solo. To complete the disguise, Leia holds a thermal detonator, knowing that the bounty hunter is famous for his love of explosives.

Built-in voice scrambler allows Leia to deceive Jabba

Bandolier packed full of explosives and detonators

Thermal detonator is a unique LEGO piece, created for this set and used in two later LEGO *Star Wars* sets

Boushh
PRINCESS IN DISGUISE

Admirable Admiral Ackbar

commands the rebel assault on the second Death Star from his flagship *Home One* (set 7754). Ackbar appears in just two LEGO sets —but his minifigure plays a pivotal part in LEGO *Star Wars* history! Ackbar is one of three Mon Calamari minifigures, but his unique commander's uniform makes him stand out.

Mon Calamari officer

This officer maintains and repairs the Home One (set 7754). His head-mold is the same as the admiral's, but his torso is unique. The dark bib protects his tan uniform from oil and dirt, while the utility belt has a pair of roomy storage pockets.

Admiral Ackbar
REBEL SUPREME COMMANDER

Solid plastic Mon Calamari head with large, bulbous eyes. The Mon Calamari officer on the ship has the same head piece, and so does Nahdar Vebb

Unique LEGO torso features a cream Mon Calamari naval jerkin over a white space suit

Home One Mon Calamari Star Cruiser (set 7754)

Admiral Ackbar coordinates the rebel assault on the second Death Star in this set. He has a swiveling and sliding command chair, and a tactical computer that can mount his lap. The set even contains his coffee cup!

Metallic command insignia denotes Ackbar's high rank

Reddish-brown webbed hands

DATA FILE

YEAR: 2009
FIRST SET: 7754 *Home One* Mon Calamari Star Cruiser
NO. OF SETS: 3
PIECES: 3
ACCESSORIES: None

Special set

Admiral Ackbar also appears in the exclusive LEGO *Star Wars* Collectible Display Set 2, which was available for one day only at the 2009 San Diego Comic-Con. Crix Madine (p.23) and Jedi Knight Luke Skywalker were also included in the set.

General Crix Madine has not always been loyal to the rebel cause—he was once an Imperial Army officer—but he is now an important leader of the Rebel Alliance with invaluable insider knowledge. His minifigure is exclusive to just two limited edition LEGO sets, but he is there when it counts—the most crucial battle in the LEGO *Star Wars* galaxy!

***Home One* Mon Calamari Star Cruiser (set 7754)**
Together with other rebel leaders Mon Mothma, Admiral Ackbar, and Lando Calrissian, General Crix Madine plans the destruction of the second Death Star in preparation for the Battle of Endor.

Exclusive
The General Madine minifigure that appears in the very rare Collectible Display Set 2 has lighter colored legs. Made for the 2009 San Diego Comic-Con, only 300 of the limited-edition sets were produced.

General Crix Madine's happy, brown-bearded face is unique to his minifigure

Collar pips denote rank

Communications badge allows Madine to contact rebel command and other leaders

Black-gloved hands

This tan torso piece was created specifically for Madine's minifigure

General Crix Madine
REBEL LEADER

DATA FILE

YEAR: 2009
FIRST SET: 7754 *Home One* Mon Calamari Star Cruiser
NO. OF SETS: 2
PIECES: 4
ACCESSORIES: None

Former senator Mon Mothma is the Supreme Commander of the Rebel Alliance. In her all-white outfit and rare white LEGO cape, her minifigure commands respect from all the rebel leaders. Mon Mothma is exclusive to the LEGO *Star Wars* set *Home One* Mon Calamari Star Cruiser (set 7754), where she discusses the latest rebel plans to defeat the Empire.

Home One Mon Calamari Star Cruiser (set 7754)
On board rebel ship *Home One*, Mon Mothma briefs the other rebel leaders about plans for the attack on the second Death Star. They gather in the command center around an orange hologram of the Death Star.

DATA FILE

YEAR: 2009
FIRST SET: 7754 *Home One* Mon Calamari Star Cruiser
NO. OF SETS: 1
PIECES: 5
ACCESSORIES: Cape

Mon Mothma
REBEL COMMANDER

Same head piece as Princess Leia, another former senator

Unique torso printed with silver Chandrilian Freedom Medal

Princess Leia wears the same white cape in Gold Leader's Y-wing Starfighter (set 9495)

Tousled hair
Mon Mothma's tousled reddish-brown hair is the same piece as that used for the Clone Wars version of Anakin Skywalker's minifigure.

STAR VARIANT
Camouflaged
This 1999 variant wears a camouflage tunic to help him blend in with the foliage on Endor. He is pursued by two scout troopers on speeder bikes (set 7128).

All in black, Luke Skywalker is hiding out with Princess Leia, Han Solo, and Chewie in a treetop Ewok Village (set 10236) on the forest moon of Endor. He certainly does a good job of staying out of sight—there are only two variants of Luke's Endor minifigure, appearing in just two LEGO *Star Wars* sets.

Hair piece
Luke's short hair is a classic LEGO piece, but only Luke Skywalker minifigures wear it in tan in LEGO *Star Wars*. However, it is seen in other themes, including LEGO® Harry Potter™ and LEGO® Soccer.

Flip face
One side of Luke's double-sided head piece has a contented smile; the other has teeth bared in a grimace.

Green lightsaber
blends in with the forest environment on Endor

Black cybernetic hand

Luke's torso
with printed tunic is unique to this minifigure

Luke Skywalker
HIDING OUT ON ENDOR

DATA FILE
YEAR: 2013
FIRST SET: 10236
Ewok Village
NO. OF SETS: 1
PIECES: 4
ACCESSORIES:
Lightsaber

Rebel leader Princess Leia Organa is preparing to fight Imperial forces on Endor. This 2013 Leia minifigure with flowing dark brown hair in long braids is exclusive to the treetop Ewok Village (set 10236). Leia's natural diplomacy skills help her befriend five Ewok minifigures who also feature in the set.

STAR VARIANT
Active on Endor
This 2009 Leia minifigure comes with The Battle of Endor (set 8038). She wears a unique camouflaged tunic and handy utility belt, but her hair remains regal—first seen on a queen in the LEGO Fantasy Era theme, it has a hole a crown can fit into.

Princess Leia
EQUIPPED FOR ENDOR

DATA FILE
YEAR: 2013
FIRST SET: 10236 Ewok Village
NO. OF SETS: 1
PIECES: 5
ACCESSORIES: Blaster

Long hair piece was first seen in dark orange on the Forest Maiden in LEGO® Collectible Minifigures Series 9

Leia wears a loose-fitting dress with a printed bow and flower details. The printing continues on the back

Unique leg piece has printed dark tan bikini briefs, underneath skirt

Ragged-edged fabric skirt in dark tan was created especially for this minifigure

STAR VARIANTS

Original Ewok

The original Wicket W. Warrick is all brown, with no printing on his head-and-torso piece. The variant appears exclusively in the 2002 set Ewok Attack (set 7139).

Hooded Ewok

This variant of Wicket's minifigure has a new orange hood on a head-and-torso piece and new printed detail on his face. It appears in the Battle of Endor set (8038) in 2009.

Wicket Wystri Warrick is a wide-eyed Ewok, native to the emerald moon of Endor. He is a minifigure of firsts in two ways: he is the first Ewok to befriend Princess Leia in The Battle of Endor (set 8038), and one of the first Ewoks to appear in LEGO form. Wicket wears a distinctive orange hood that sets him apart from other LEGO Ewoks.

DATA FILE

YEAR: 2013
FIRST SET: 10236 Ewok Village
NO. OF SETS: 1
PIECES: 3
ACCESSORIES: Spear

Wicket's dark orange hood has stitching where he once tore it

Detailed face printing is first seen on the 2009 design

LEGO Ewoks

Along with his fellow Ewok warrior Paploo, Wicket was one of the earliest LEGO Ewoks. Chief Chirpa followed in 2009, while Logray and Tokkat appeared in 2011.

Unique head-and-torso sandwich-board piece has textured fur

Ewoks are small in stature, so Wicket has short, unposeable LEGO legs

Wicket W. Warrick

EWOK WARRIOR

27

Editors Pamela Afram, Hannah Dolan, Clare Hibbert, Shari Last, Julia March, Victoria Taylor, Ellie Barton, Matt Jones, Clare Millar, and Rosie Peet
Senior Designers Jo Connor, and David McDonald
Senior Slipcase Designer Mark Penfound
Designers Elena Jarmoskaite, Pamela Shiels, Mark Richards, Anne Sharples, Jon Hall, and Stefan Georgiou
Pre-Production Producer Kavita Varma
Senior Producer Lloyd Robertson
Managing Editor Paula Regan
Design Manager Guy Harvey
Creative Manager Sarah Harland
Art Director Lisa Lanzarini
Publisher Julie Ferris
Publishing Director Simon Beecroft

Consultants Jon Hall and Ace Kim
Additional minifigures photographed by Gary Ombler

First American Edition, 2016
Publsihed in the United States by
DK Publishing 345 Hudson Street,
New York, New York 10014
DK, a Division of Penguin Random
House LLC

Contains content previously
published in LEGO® Star Wars™
*Character Encyclopedia, Updated
and Expanded* (2015)

Page design copyright © 2016
Dorling Kindersley Limited

002–298872–Jan/17

LEGO, the LEGO logo, the Brick
and Knob configurations, and the
Minifigure are trademarks of the
LEGO Group. © 2016 The LEGO
Group. All rights reserved.
Produced by Dorling Kindersley
Limited under license from the
LEGO Group.

A catalog record for this book is
available from the Library of Congress.

ISBN 978-5-0010-1395-2

Printed in China

www.LEGO.com/starwars
www.dk.com

A WORLD OF IDEAS:
SEE ALL THERE IS TO KNOW

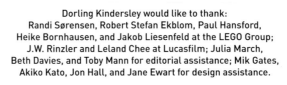

Dorling Kindersley would like to thank:
Randi Sørensen, Robert Stefan Ekblom, Paul Hansford,
Heike Bornhausen, and Jakob Liesenfeld at the LEGO Group;
J.W. Rinzler and Leland Chee at Lucasfilm; Julia March,
Beth Davies, and Toby Mann for editorial assistance; Mik Gates,
Akiko Kato, Jon Hall, and Jane Ewart for design assistance.